OBSESSION

Louis Begley ◆ David Bradley
Robert Olen Butler ◆ Thomas Flanagan
Ernest Gaines ◆ Barry Hannah ◆ Maureen Howard
Jayne Anne Phillips ◆ George Plimpton ◆ Francine Prose
Vikram Seth ◆ Mary Lee Settle ◆ Ntozake Shange
Elizabeth Spencer ◆ Scott Spencer

Quill & Brush
1994

ISBN 1-883060-02-8 Signed edition
ISBN 1-883060-03-6 Paperwraps edition

Quill & Brush
Box 5365
Rockville, MD 20848

Introduction

This little book was the script for the Fifth PEN/Faulkner Gala, held on October 2, 1993, at the Folger Shakespeare Library in Washington, D.C. The writers who took part had been asked to sing for their supper — and for fellow writers' suppers as well, since the proceeds of the Gala go a long way toward supporting the PEN/Faulkner Awards in Fiction.

One by one, in alphabethical order, the writers took the podium to offer up their remarks on the evening's theme, "Obsession." There had been some good-natured grumbling about this topic, with wisecracks about a certain perfume, and about the three-minute time limit, which no one observed (though backstage, behind the heavy crimson curtain, the writers waiting their turn timed each presentation). The whole enterprise reminded some of the writers of those periods in high school English when the entire class had to sit down and write on a set theme.

The written text conveys the wit and imagination that were brought to bear; but the physical presence of the speakers, the tug of their voices, the spell each writer cast in the intimate Shakespeare Theater — all this merely lingers in the white space on the printed pages. For those of us in the audience, the effect was exhilarating and kaleidoscopic, for no sooner had one writer fixed a vivid image then the next came forward to rearrange the crystals and hold them up to a different light.

Almost in spite of itself, since the writers sought primarily to entertain, this program showed exactly what writers have always been able to bring to a deliberation. Especially in a city like Washington, where abstractions rule and language is mostly institutional, the particularity and strong individuality of each presentation was startling, almost shocking. Here were men and women willing to speak for themselves, and only for themselves, men and women who did not hide behind abstractions and wanted no truck with institutions. Their authority came from another, more powerful source.

On behalf of PEN/Faulkner, I thank you for buying this book, for your purchase makes you a benefactor. Our thanks are also due to the Ford Motor Company, primary sponsors of the Gala for five years running. For the writers who gave their time and talent, I hope this book will be a permanent reminder of their good will and generosity.

Stephen Goodwin
President
PEN/Faulkner Foundation

Obsession

LOUIS BEGLEY

Louis Begley

Louis Begley

The children were the first to notice. As soon as they saw me do it, they pointed with their fingers and tittered. Then they told my wife about it. I would hear them all laughing until tears ran down their cheeks, her laughter always the brightest, like a crystal bell, never failing to thrill me even when it's at my expense.

It became official on my fiftieth birthday. Visions of perfectly honed #2 Ticonderoga pencils had been dancing in my head. I had been hoping for a rechargeable sharpener. But as soon as the cake had been cut, before I could herd them together for a family snapshot, they presented me with the Stradivarius of brooms, a yellow ribbon tied around the bright red handle, a red one pleated in its head of blond straw. No explanation was needed. It was the perfect gift for a man whose obsession is sweeping.

How had it started? In Long Island. We had acquired a house with a summer room that looks like a yogurt factory. The floor was made of flagstones. At its edge, covering the native sand, were gray and white pebbles. For similar aesthetic reasons, the builder had sowed more pebbles in the space between the flagstones lining the part that leads to the pool. Only I was nimble enough to walk in and out of the summer room or on the path without disturbing the pebbles. Under the feet of my family or guests, the pebbles scattered, or, worse yet invaded the surface of the flagstones. I watched warily for this breakout of disorder. At first I would brush the pebbles back to where they were intended to be stealthily, with my bare toes. Soon, I was no longer able to contain myself. Indifferent to my audience, I would neaten quite openly, sweeping the pebbles to the circumference of the summer room or the interstices in the pool path. The stooped, melancholy and stubborn figure—broom in hand—that's me, the solitary sweeper of Long Island's South Fork.

What does it mean? Clean sweep? Swept away? Sweep under the rug? None of these metaphors fits my grand obsession. To sweep is to restore order. To return to an imagined world of pristine innocence. So I ride my broomstick in search of a stasis of perfection where each thing, breathless and suspended, is beautifully just where it should be.

DAVID BRADLEY

David Bradley

Wow! Three minutes on obsession in Washington, D.C. on a night when the Skins are playing. Is that enough?

You know, doing this assignment represented a research problem. I mean where do you go to do three minutes worth of research, on anything, let alone about obsession? Where do you find inspiration? I went to the video store. And in the clean, well-lighted aisles of my local Brain Rotter, I discovered that the most popular of our popular films, which is to say the ones that weren't there—just the boxes were there—had obsession as a theme. Interestingly though, it seemed that the object of the obsession didn't matter. Obsession itself was the rub. Nearly every cassette box promised me a tragic tale in which some ungovernable demand was the flaw that led to a burnt-out

BMW in every parking structure and a rabbit, rather than a chicken, in every pot.

Well, I thought here is my news. In modern America for all our supposed excesses, we loathe obsession. We fear it and generate graphic, cautionary tales against it. So I noted down a few phrases and went back to better work, in the course of which I happened on the following quote:

> It was heard in every sound and seen in every thing. It was ever present to torment me with a sense of my wretched condition. I saw nothing without seeing it, heard nothing without hearing it, felt nothing without feeling it. It looked from every star. It smiled in every calm, breathed in every wind and moved in every storm. I often found myself regretting my own existence and wishing myself dead.

Gadzooks! thought I. That's an obsession. The trouble was, it was Frederick Douglass writing about his lust for freedom. This gave me considerable pause, for Douglass has always been one of my idols. Well, not an idol, a role model— I don't want to sound obsessed or anything. But when I was young, I wanted to grow up to look like him, and later though male pattern baldness put paid to that ambition, I continued to admire him. But now I realized Fred Douglass had been an obsessive, wild for freedom long before he tasted it. And his obsession was destructive; his lust caused him to mock and assault his superiors, to default on lawful contracts, to abandon his pregnant lover, to defy the laws of state and nation. The message from Brain Rotter video was clear. It would never do now, in this America, to idolize a man like that.

Well I'll compress the mental agonies that followed. Suffice to say I could not give Douglass up, and predictably I descended into madness from whence I began to judge the quick and the dead. The Founders of this nation, for example, now appeared to me not as patriots, but zealots, risking lives, fortunes and sacred honors to confront a power against which they had to go toe to toe because their heads would not have reached their opponent's ankles. Indeed they challenged not merely a nation but the natural order of the universe—the Great Chain of being—God himself. Nay, they declared, there is no chain. All are created equal. Clearly, these were obsessive madmen. And I in my madness loved them, not for their wisdom, but for their obsessive insanity. And I loathed the eight who regained their senses, and with others, framed a constitution that in the interest of domestic tranquillity compromised equality, and counted some men and women but three-fifths. And I became suspicious—yes, I'll say it—paranoid, about our current politics, this so-called spirit of compromise that is the antithesis of obsession. Pray tell me, citizen, what is so wonderful about consensus building, about having everything on the table? What would we have been now if independence had been negotiable? Oh, we'd be covered by a national health plan, true. But we'd be British, or Canadians at best.

Today we seek the middling middle ground in everything, responding less to principles than to interest. Why, just last week I heard some government official say, “This is not a crusade. It’s a pragmatic effort to see freedom take hold where it will help us the most.” Is that what our rebellion has come to? Are we no longer the apostles of freedom to all, but brokers of freedom to those who are most useful to us? What’s wrong with a crusade for freedom? I mean, we have crusades against tobacco. But, (I see the red light is on, so let me quickly say) I don’t mean any of this. I’m not obsessed or anything. But since Fred Douglass doesn’t fit the times, I thought I’d try Rush Limbaugh.

ROBERT OLEN BUTLER

Robert Olen Butler

Even before I knew there was another part of girls that would one day whisper to me, that would call me over and over, there was the machine in my uncle's shoe store and there was Karen Granger, and she was on my mind all the time. And I somehow knew that I had to get her to put her feet in the machine.

My uncle's was the last shoe store in Granite City, Illinois, to put in an X-ray machine to check the fit. And as soon as it was ready, I went to Karen and brought her to the shop. She had on her black Mary Janes and white lace anklets, and she went up on the step and put her feet in the slots and my heart was beating furiously as I stepped up beside her, for there were two view ports, and together we looked at the bones in her feet. I lifted my arm and I put it around her, cupping her far shoulder in my hand.

"Wiggle your toes," I said. She did. And to this day, though I am now 48 years old, there have been few moments in my life as intimate as the sight of Karen Granger's actual bones; her actual articulated bones with their shape visible to me, the shape that had been secret even when she stood barefoot in the grass of her front yard bossing me and giving me an excuse to keep my eyes cast down. She wiggled her toes in the green glow of the X-ray, and she let me keep my arm around her and she began to hum softly.

As I think of her now it seems true, what I just said, that the intimacy of that moment with Karen Granger in 1955, in the eleventh year of my life, was rarely matched in all the years since. And yet, I did not think of her again for decades. She did not begin to hum again in my head until a few months ago, on a trip to Puerto Vallarta, and then she came with a newspaper article on X-rays and health, and I let the paper fall from my hand by my canvas chair on the beach.

She came briefly with that and then much more strongly an hour later with the smell of shoe leather in a shop in the hotel, the smell and a glimpse of the bare feet of a slim blond woman wearing a towel knotted at her hip, slipping past me without a glance.

I can't remember what song it was that Karen hummed as I pressed her against me, though trying to remember it distracted me in the Mexican shoe shop. I did not look again at the blond woman, but fixed on the buckle of a sandal in my hand and I tried to make the humming shape itself into a tune. And now of course I understand it's not the tune I really want to know. I want to know why she hummed. Did she know her bones were beautiful to me? Did she feel the same intimacy? Did she wait for me to ask to put my own feet in the machine? This is the thought that bothers me. I wish now, wish devoutly, that I had whispered to her, "My turn," and I had put my feet in the machine, and she had seen my bones.

THOMAS FLANAGAN

Thomas Flanagan

I was delighted to have been asked back to PEN/ Faulkner, which seemed to me one of those rare literary occasions which are both elegant and human. Ever since April, when PEN/Faulkner asked me to join with you and talk about obsession for three minutes, I have been able to think of little else.

I went first of course to the dictionary. Not the *OED*. I had misplaced the magnifying glass, and in any event, using it always arouses my latent feelings of social inferiority. A friend many years ago inherited a full set from his father, and I always imagine him strolling to his shelf while I crouch over microscopic type. I did go, though, to its admirable abridgment, the *Oxford Universal Dictionary*, where I discovered of course that all my life it or I had been using the word incorrectly. The word obsession derives, I was instructed, from the Latin *obsidere* and meant originally "to besiege," as a fortress is besieged or invested. And thence, says the dictionary, actuation by the devil or an evil spirit from without. And thence, finally, from that, the action of any influence, notion or fixed idea which persistently assails or vexes. But this ran very counter to my notion that an obsession arises from within and seizes upon the external. A man obsessed by the notion that he is the reincarnation of Napoleon is not influenced toward that big leap by a chance visit to Waterloo, or by marriage to a woman named Josephine; it is quite the other way around. His obsession leads him to seek out the battlefield that he may relive an old sorrow, and he pays court to a woman who bears the appropriate name.

I turned to *Webster's Third*, which of course dismissed the besetting activities of devils or spirits as obsolete, *obs*. *Obs* is an abbreviation which in *Webster's Third* always carries a chilling whiff of contempt. *Webster's* settles instead for "a persistent and disturbing intrusion of, or anxious and inescapable preoccupation with a feeling, especially if known to be unreasonable." This seemed even worse. Obsessions are indeed persistent but they need not be disturbing or a cause of anxiety, nor something from which one vainly seeks relief. Surely it all depends on the nature of the obsession. And the more I reflected on it, the more hostile seemed that word "unreasonable." Unreasonable to whom? It seems a bit nasty of external reality first to implant the obsession in the sufferer's mind and then to condemn that mind for accepting it. Dictionaries claim to be neutral judges of language, but in fact they are subtle casuists. And in fact they are subtle casuists directed against writers and artists in general, who believe that their central energies arise from within, and then confront the without.

After these two, I had no need to consult their lesser and more recent rivals, but something unreasonable and obsessive drove me on. The *American College Dictionary* speaks of the besetting or dominating action or influence of a persistent feeling, idea "or the like." One turns to a dictionary for precision, and is fobbed off with an airy wave of the editorial hand, "or the like!"

The *American Heritage Dictionary* is the most modern, with hundreds of line drawings and little reproductions in the margin. I had hoped, as I turned to the O's to find a drawing modeled upon Fuseli or Goya of an actual obsession, crouched upon a skull and battering for entrance. I was disappointed but was able to learn that of recent years, the verb "to obsess" has acquired an intransitive usage. For illustration, the *Heritage* turns not to Walter Pater or Evelyn Waugh or Vladimir Nabokov. Instead it goes right to stylistic headquarters, to Scott Turow himself, one of whose novels contains the line "She's dead but you're still obsessing."

After that, it took me the better part of two days to find the magnifying glass, but was it worth the effort and the dust? When the *OED* needs an illustration it turns to the splendidly named Hubert Crackenthorpe, a decadent of the English 1890s and a justly forgotten one, who is quoted as having said, "The thought of death began to haunt him until it became a constant obsession." One does not quarrel easily with the OED, but surely all obsessions are constant?

My task, fortunately, has only begun. Roget's and Webster's Thesaurus list among synonyms: fixations, fascination, phantom, craze, delusion, mania, infatuation, fixed idea, compulsion and (perhaps Mr. Turow's contribution) hang-up. I am now in the process of hunting down these words and their shadings and colorations. It is a task before which everything else seems unreasonably to be fading away.

ERNEST GAINES

Ernest Gaines

An obsession of mine concerns a half-acre of land in south-central Louisiana. This plot of land is surrounded by sugarcane fields on all sides, some of the rows coming within 20 feet of it. This plot of land is where my ancestors have been buried the past 100 years, where most of the people I knew as a child are now buried. This is Riverlake plantation, Point Coupee Parish, Oscar, Louisiana.

The first 15-and-a-half years of my life were spent on this place. My ancestors for over a hundred years planted the sugarcane here, hoed the sugarcane, plowed it, cut it and when it was time, hauled it to the mills. They, like so many others who worked this land are buried here in unmarked graves because they could not afford the headstones.

A hundred years ago, the land was owned by one man who designated that the land would be a cemetery for the people on that plantation, but he did not give it to them, nor would he let them buy it. Today the land is owned by 16 people who live all over the country and probably different parts of the world, some of which I'm sure have never visited the plantation or know anything about the cemetery which lies there. Yet it is their land, and those who are buried there do not own even six foot of the ground.

Many rural cemeteries have been destroyed all over this country, and day and night I worry that the same fate may happen to this one. There is no law in the state of Louisiana that I am aware of that says it cannot be done. My wife and I and several friends from my childhood are trying to find a way to get control of the land. We have contacted lawyers to work with us and presently we are keeping the place clean of overgrowth, because that is one excuse landowners and developers use to plow under cemeteries. "We didn't know that one was there."

At a recent interview, I was asked where would I like to be buried and I answered that I'd like to be in the same place where my ancestors are. The interviewer asked me what would I like on my headstone and I said, "To lie with those who have no marks." These are the people for whom I wrote letters as a child, read their letters because many of them could not read nor could they write. Many of them had to go into the fields before they had a chance to go to school. Yet they're the ones responsible for my being here tonight. Not only did they encourage me to stay in school, but they, and only they, have been the source of all of my writings. I've said many times before that my novels, my short stories, are just continuations of the letters that I started writing for them some 50 years ago, and since I've tried to say something about their lives on paper—their joy, their sorrows, their love, their fears, their pride, their compassion—I think it is only my duty now to do as much as I can to see that they lie in peace forever.

BARRY HANNAH

Barry Hannah

Farewells

Having held a teaching job off and on for 25 years without dispatching a single piece of scholarship, I thought I might read for this high occasion a brief commentary on a passage by Samuel Beckett, the master of farewells. Especially since I have said deep farewells lately just here in the last two years, to my father, my mother, and our own dear cat Billy—a gentleman fat, gray and white who took care of baby kittens not even of his own paternity all sweet nine years of his life. Wounded by a horse I think, Billy could not even rightly meow, yet he curled there in the monkey grass at the back steps, or slept in the laundry basket with great optimism. Farewell again, Pappy, Mammy and Billy, sic transit, Mr. Beckett, too. Farewell again old friend, quiet, strange and exact, who wrote:

> All the old ways led to this, all the old windings. The stairs with never a landing that you screw yourself up clutching the rail, counting the steps, the fever of shortest ways under the long lids of sky, the wild country roads where your dead walk beside you on the dark shingle that turning for the last time again to the lights of the little town, the appointments kept and the appointments broken, all the delights of urban and rural change of place, all the exitus and reditus closed and ended. All led to this, to this gloaming where a middle-aged man sits stroking his snout waiting for the first dawn to break...

To which this writer says yes, with abundance, stroking my snout in wild thanks for the beautiful lonesomeness this life of writing has afforded me and most grateful to my listeners.

At a certain time in life, something falls inward. You can almost hear the shudder in your chest. You'll see many things for the last time. Almost everything becomes elegiac, so you must watch very carefully, my friends, and touch these things with tenderness.

MAUREEN HOWARD

Maureen Howard

Maureen Howard

For Meg Greenfield

My dears, I have never been what you suggest. The idea that I should be beholden to, let's say, the erratic splashing of a killer whale or wish to display upon my palms the bloody nail holes of the crucifixion, displeases me. Displeasure—the very word gives you a clue to the sort of unruffled woman I am. Neither sinner, nor saint; I've not known the corrupting passion of the mad captain nor the ecstasy of the little virgin bleeding, as it were, from the wrong places. Neither a loser nor a winner be: give me a pail of quarters, face me off with a one arm bandit, I will not waste one coin in a frenzy of hope against hope that three identical cherries or lemons or limes will bing, bing, bing into place. Unless, of course, it is love—first, second or fourth—you intend by obsession, those hormonal overdrives, seizures of the heart we are prone to, more than passing fancy, passing nevertheless, within the natural order. If that's all you mean, I've been there, but I suspect you are after something else. Confession is begged by the unholy word. Idolatry? Witchcraft? I have no such history, and must conjure for you a harmless story.

Two girls, they shall be nameless, but in the days of girls at a girlish college sharing a room, both given to dreaming life into art, small life they knew: it was for them foreign films, gay posters of Lautrec and Marie Cassatt, the strenuous modern dance. Chekov and Charles Trenez, Parsifal, twin sets, Cizano were all too lovely. In their flannel nightgowns they wrote, often late into the night—poems. You'd know it was poetry had you ever known them, moony and innocent as they were. One wrote heroic couplets, villanelles—an angular girl tucked up in smooth blankets, versifying in her loose leaf notebook. Adept at enjambment, caesura, she won all the prizes with her poems which were of things—statues and paintings, landscape, the weather.

Across the room, a frowsy girl ate cookies in her bed. Propped with a snoutless bear, a napless creature, she sighed, laughed, rumpling her quilt, scribbling, erasing in a red book, a silly book it was, let me tell you, cheap red cloth embossed with improbable daisies and whatever was written on those pages, written with those sighs, hums, elicited a sucking of breath in pain or was it pleasure? The red book was never offered, never to be seen one girl to another, that secrecy an affront to the poetess with the prizes who wondered what faltering rhymes, dear-diary stuff might be hidden from her in the red book with its lock, yes the teeny lock with teeny key secreted somewhere in the room like a child's game taunting her to find it, the red book the last thing she saw at night, the last thing she heard the feeble scratch of its key, its frayed edges the first slight of the morning mocking her own neat couplets or quatrains to be typed on a slippery, sleek Olivetti, until on a gray evening, alone, naked, come quick from the shower, the red blank book, for that's all it was, fell at her feet not like a lover, and she tore at the flimsy lock to see the smudges, crumbs on the page to find there (have you guessed it?) words spun free in their lines, the wild surmise, journey work of the stars—without artifice and, yes, without things, not a trace of teddy bear or common daisy.

In a precarious balance, the girlish scale of things, it was like first looking into Chapman's Homer; Emerson opening, my god, Leaves of Grass; coming upon a sacred scrap of Amherst's blest spinster. Having broken the lock, to burn the red book? The ashes, the stench. Toss it then in the dormitory trash where its cover would scream for retrieval? No. Run in bathrobe and bare feet—cold, bitter cold—sink it in the sludge of Paradise Pond, wash away words, blank the blank book.

Frowsy still, rumpled—the woman reads from her collected works. They hang from the rafters. The great show, I am told, is to hear her proclaim from memory her earliest poems, each line soft and clear, exhibiting in the spoken moment the delight in her discovery of the lost book, the indelible words. You will have to make do with this transparent fable. I'm sorry if you wanted de Sade's sexual exhaustions, Loyola's gift of tears: I write grocery lists, my dears, thank you notes, reviews, the occasional essay.

I have never been possessed by words.

JAYNE ANNE PHILLIPS

Jayne Anne Phillips

Obsession: A Simple Story

We live on a rural road in a forgotten place somewhere in the 1950s. My mother has gone to college nights until at last she has a job as a teacher of six-year-olds. Many of the kids are brought in on buses from the hollows and settlements that crop up along the dirt roads. Our own road is a concrete two-lane that runs past open fields and isolated houses. One of those houses is a narrow bungalow perched at the crest of a hill. It sits up on blocks, has no foundation. We call it the shed. My mother says it ought to be against the law to rent a house like that to anybody. But people move into and out of the shed. Or it is empty whole seasons, winters mostly, when it must be barely habitable.

My brothers and I go to the same school where my mother teaches, but sometimes we ride the bus. This year, when I'm ten years old, the bus stops at the shed and two scrawny boys walk out alone. They climb onto the bus and stand still for a moment in the aisle, looking at the rest of us. They have the fragile, porcelain skin that seems to characterize neglected kids from the country, and sores at their lips, and ill-fitting clothes. But these boys have their hair slicked back tall, Elvis style, and their features are fine and sharp like those of little foxes. They take us in with their pale blue eyes, scent the air. Then the older one, who must be eight, puts his arm around the younger, and they sit down. Soon I'm hearing about the little one, Nathan, from my mother. He's in her class. He's one of the two or three she takes to the lunchroom in the mornings before school even starts. She finds them something to eat, and the cooks look the other way. She takes clothes to school for Nathan, too. And towels, and soap. He comes to school smelling of urine. Sometimes he has accidents. She brings his dirty clothes home and washes them, and takes them back to school. Somehow Nathan knows who I am, that I am her daughter, and I see him standing alone in the long noon hours, watching me.

My mother tells me Nathan's mother takes off for weeks, riding around in a tour bus with some country singer. I've seen her downtown on Saturdays, a woman the size of a little girl, petite and foxish like the boys. She wears tight gold lamé pants, spangly earrings, and her brown hair hangs below her hips. The kids seem to take care of themselves. Apparently there's another boy, younger than Nathan. Sometimes we see them all outside in the field behind the shed, but we never see the parents.

One day Nathan has another accident in class and my mother takes him into the teachers' restroom to help him change his clothes. She's preoccupied, having left the inexperienced student teacher in charge. She fills the sink with warm soapy water and hands him a washcloth. Then she actually looks at him. She's seen marks on him before, but today there's no mistaking the long bands of discolored bruises across his back and hips and legs. She asks him, "Nathan, what happened to you?" And he doesn't make up another story about falling off a fence. He tells her in his soft flat voice, "Daddy beat me with a board." My mother takes him back to class, then calls the county welfare office. She tells them "I'm not sending him back to that house. Either you find a place for him or I'll take him home with me." In fact he does come home with us. We give him chocolate milk and graham crackers while my mother makes more phone calls. She convinces a kindly older couple, Hank and Christine, friends of my father's, to take Nathan, and they sign themselves up as foster parents.

I know a little about a lot of people in the town by listening to adults talk. I know a little about Hank and Christine. They're childless. Hank is big and ruddy with a shock of white hair. Years ago he had a problem; he nearly drank himself to death. Now the town says of them, "She stood right by him, and for once it worked." It all seems to work tonight. Hank and Christine come for supper as though we're all a big family. Then they take Nathan home to their spare room, to a teddy bear and a new coverlet printed with cowboys and clouds. Over the next three weeks they take him to a circus in a neighboring town, and shopping for a winter parka. He has a new pair of boots with stitching on the sides, like cowboys wear. And at recess at school he stands with his brother on the playground. He brings the brother over to me nearly every day, silently, the two of them with their fists in their pockets. I wonder if the brother is angry because Nathan was taken away, but he doesn't seem angry. He inspects Nathan's new boots and seems eager to talk, as though he wants to make a good impression. I think about the first time I saw him on the bus, the look on his wary face and his arm around Nathan. He had someone to protect. Now he's not sure.

The bell rings and the playground begins to empty. The boys go off in different directions, the brother hesitating, shuffling his feet. The look he gives me over his shoulder is one of such grudging hope and uncertainty that I feel angry at my mother. Angry that she hasn't rescued him, too. Rescued all the kids like him, who after all only have each other. But soon I hear that Nathan's back with his family, that there wasn't enough evidence to keep him out of the home. Soon the family moves on, disappears. The shack of a house stands empty again.

One day in the spring I'm riding my bicycle past and surprise myself by turning onto the dirt track that leads across scrub grass behind Nathan's house. I stand beside the rickety back porch, which is about as broad as a sidewalk. There's a view of fields, and the stream beyond, and the wooded hills. This is what Nathan saw, and over that way to the right he saw my house, a brick ranch house with trikes and bikes in the yard, as far away as the moon. Strangely, there are no windows in the shed at all, but there's a circular window with a glass pane, like a peep hole, in the back door. So I look through. It's months since they left, but the floor is strewn with objects as though they ran out yesterday, dropping things. A shoe. Torn magazines. A cot-sized mattress, ripped and propped up so that its contents seemed to spill out in a damaged froth. I can see the wood stove squarely in the middle of the little room, hulking, its awkward pipe piercing the ceiling. I look for something of Nathan—the boots, or the coverlet, crumpled into a corner, no longer sky blue—but nothing is there. He's taken it all with him.

GEORGE PLIMPTON

George Plimpton

I am obsessed by fireworks. I have been so since childhood—astonished by the alchemic wonder of touching a match to inert matter and have it rise and perform its miracle of color and concussion in the night sky. I think my obsession is because I'm a writer, who, unlike the pyrotechnician, rarely has the opportunity to realize the effect of his or her work on a reader. The English novelist John Mortimer once told me of a writer friend of his who got on the tube at Piccadilly and discovered that the young woman on the seat opposite was reading a book of his. He knew that 40 or 50 pages from where she was reading, there was a scene which would surely produce a laugh. So rather than getting off at Green Park, his original destination, he stayed on until the end of the line at Cockfosters, waiting for the laugh. It never came.

The writer identifies with Mallarmé, the bemoan of the blank page that faces him or her every day, the appalling difficulty of decorating it with words. Compare the fireworks man who touches a flame to a fuse and within seconds the "oohs" and the "aahs" rise from the hillside from those in wonder at what he has done in the night sky.

And how fortunate he is with his black canvas of the night sky—the faint and insignificant stars, comets of minuscule aesthetic value, a moon which only shows its one face—and how eagerly he decorates it with manmade brush strokes, fat comets, rainbow-hued stars, mad whirligigs...doing better with the heavens than the gods themselves.

The Chinese, very likely because they discovered the earliest pyrothechnical ingredients, are wondrously imaginative in naming their fireworks. A tag accompanying a shell from the Orient will read "The Monkeys Enter the Heavenly Temple and Drive Out the Tiger." Alas, our more prosaic retailers change this to "Sky Monkeys." "Humming Birds Blossom over the Yangtze and Blot Out the Moon" is muted to "Colored Birds."

In my later years, the octogenarian phase, I would like to become a fireworks shell namer, my fame such that I am called to China every autumn to name their newest produce. I step off a train in a distant province carrying a small suitcase. I am met by officials who bow very low. At the firing site a chair is brought out with a soft cushion in it. Dusk. And then the night sky comes with its miserable display of stars—insignificant, immaterial, no moon —the perfect canvas. I'm handed a pen and a sheet of rice paper. The first shell of the night flutters up, a comet tale, then a cascade of blue stars. I am lost in thought. "The Blue Ox Comes Down the Turnpike?" No, that will not do. "I am not inspired," I tell them. "Send it up again."

That night will be the only time I put pen to paper until autumn comes around and I am summoned once again.

FRANCINE PROSE

Francine Prose

Francine Prose

In many ways there is nothing more boring than obsession. That tiny pinpoint of white light glittering on the horizon, reducing the whole world around it to grayness and general blur. Its qualities are fixation, monotony, repetition. It's yet another psychoactive drug, like alcohol or LSD, that looks better from the inside than it ever does from the outside. Our best friends are tired of hearing about it, that thing or person we desperately want, that muddy center we poor, possessed oxen trudge round and round in circles.

The interesting exceptions are the obsessions of great obsessives—Joan of Arc, Napoleon, Freud, Columbus, Mother Theresa, Saint Simeon Stylites sitting 30 years on a pole in the desert; an extreme and very early piece of religious performance art.

And what's more interesting even than that is the mysterious way in which obsessions great and small are alchemically turned into art. Of course, this is a great mystery and defies explanation. Kafka wrote to his father, "Everything I wrote was about you," and it was everything, but only a very small part of Gregor Samsa's short sad life as a cockroach. Marcel Proust building with tea cakes, and with a particular hat that a particular duchess wore to a particular party and constructing a model of nothing less than time itself. How does he differ exactly from the little boy whose parents are sick with worry because he is maniacally building with Legos and never goes out to play with his friends?

Every artist is an obsessive. Some are eccentric, like Joseph Cornell. Some of us are hidden about it. Some wallow in it, like Kafka. We become obsessed with writers whose obsessions match our own, so one year it may be Collette, and the next, George Orwell.

Writers write from obsession, and to learn what their obsessions are. I seem, for example, to be obsessed with household pets and weddings, two subjects I think are beside the point in what I think is my conscious life. I always imagine Flaubert working for months to come up with the perfect gift for Emma Bovary to give her lover; Tolstoy breaking the printer's plates and rewriting Anna Karenina.

If there is an obsession that writers have in common, it's the obsession with truth and perfection, that maddened fixation on every word is the hallmark of a real writer. Writers are like those screamers who yell at you in the street, shouting the same phrases, the same words again and again and again, convinced that someone will stop and reply if they can only just get it right.

VIKRAM SETH

Vikram Seth

The Freckle

I had expected Dr. Lee in Dermatology to be Chinese, but he turned out to be a very large white man. He looked carefully at the freckle on my lip and asked me to strip to my waist. Then he said he would have to remove the tissue surgically the next day.

"But it's just a freckle, Doctor."

"Yes, that's what I think, too," he replied cheerfully. "Tomorrow, then. 2:15."

"But Doctor, can't it wait a week? I've had this for months and my Macroeconomics exams are coming soon. It'll disturb my schedule."

“Well, the quicker the better, I think. That way we’ll feel safe.”

“But why this operation?”

“No, no. Not an operation, just a procedure.”

“What might it be,” I said, “this freckle?”

“Now, don’t jump the gun,” said Dr. Lee, smiling.

“Well, what might it be?”

“Well there’s a small chance it might be what we call... well, what we like to call a melanoma.”

That sounded unthreatening, even musical. Melanoma. I repeated the word to myself several times as I biked back to my room. Then I went back to studying the effects of monetary policy on the labor market.

On the next day, after the incision, at which the doctor's eyes were grave and he mentioned the word "biopsy," I looked up "melanoma" in the university library and, to the alarm of people sitting near me, began to gasp. I remembered the expression on the doctor's face and realized that there was a good chance I was going to die, and die soon. I went to the bathroom and stared at the small, bandaged patch on my lip, then into my unfamiliar eyes.

The biopsy results would be obtained in four days' time. I sat under a eucalyptus tree when I should have been in class and wept in the broad Californian sunlight. I wept for myself and for my family so far away and for the terror, rather than the pain, of my disease. How would it progress over me and through me? That evening I read more about it, and my panic grew. The word "melanoma," which still sounded almost consolingly musical, took over my days and nights. I could not sleep. I couldn't bear to study, and I avoided my friends. At night I sat in my room, turned off the lights, and looked at a section of the sky. Neither Mozart nor masturbation helped. One terrified me further with its unsparing loveliness, the other proved infeasible. I clasped my arms to my chest and shook. I examined my body for further spots, but I had never charted a map of my own constellations, and I did not know what was new. I hardly ate, and when I did, I ate ravenously. All the headlines of the newspapers reflected my condition.

Suddenly in the darkness a great clarity came. I would go home to India. I would do what I had often longed in my homesickness to do. I would throw out my study of Economics and go home and write poetry in the last year of my life. What this poetry would be I did not know, but it would be borne of fear and hope and sorrow, and a reconciling of myself with the universe. I would make sure that when I died, those that I loved would not be left with a sense that I had not lived.

The next day I was told that it was indeed just a freckle. "They are quite similar, you know," said Dr. Lee. "Structurally, I mean." I promptly returned to the study of monetary policy and the labor market, and remained in economics for several years. I could not even remember when writing this whether the freckle had been on my upper or lower lip till I recalled how I had stared at that stranger's face in the mirror. It was the upper lip.

MARY LEE SETTLE

Mary Lee Settle

Mary Lee Settle

The most common obsession, one we have usually survived by the time we are 21, is falling in love. Alas, with some of us, the experience goes on and on and on. It is not love. They are as different literally as day and night. Love is of the day, daily, survives in lovely light, reality, acceptance of one's fellow beings. Falling in love is alone and of the night, dreams, insomnia, hopes, fears and above all, the question, "Why?"

I do not propose to say anything wise about falling in love. There is little wise to say. I fall in love every three years. My husband is very understanding. At least I think he is. But his obsession is chess, which is after all a war game between partners in which you win by checking your mate. He can read the signs, though, from long experience—the staring into space, the waiting, the deterioration of the food from gourmet cooking to what we call "plates of stuff."

Like all falling in love, it begins with an image, evasive and uninvited. The lover moves into my mind as a squatter would move into a house, always at first unknown. Cruel? Oh, often. Like Jim in the song who doesn't send me pretty flowers and makes me, God knows, wait the lonely hours. Sometimes, not often, the image is like Juliet's beauteous flower, formed and glowing. But even that can be suppressed at first so easily by interference, demands, the human voices that wake us and we drown. So I begin to question this intruder, and go on questioning. Know, because it's happened before, that I have received a gift and a burden for which I have not asked. Like Jacob and the angel, I cannot let it go until it blesses me with the answer to "Why?" Why has it happened? What does it want of me? The months pass, sometimes the years—once 28 years of this sustained illusion. The image has taken up residence, becomes familiar, more so than daily life. The physical horizon narrows to a single room, the dream horizon of my love expands beyond oceans, empires and time. And finally the questions are answered as well as I can. The work is done. I have been blessed and can let go.

The book is finished. I can reenter the human race, be quiet, content, love daily life, cook well and cultivate, as Candide learned, my garden.

I hope every time against hope, of course, that it will never, never happen again, which is as obsessive an illusion as the initial image. Sometimes I'm asked innocently why I chose to write. I didn't choose it. Like a lover, it chose me. Nobody but a fool, or an obsessive, would work so hard for such low pay.

NTOZAKE SHANGE

Ntozake Shange

This is an obsession of a character of mine who's a favorite character of mine. She appears in several things, in some stories and two plays and in the next novel in different manifestations. She only has the same name. Her name is Lilly.

I'm gonna simply brush my hair. Rapunzel, pull your tresses back into the tower and Lady Godiva, give up horseback riding! I'm gonna alter my social and professional life dramatically. I will brush a hundred strokes in the morning, a hundred strokes midday and a hundred strokes before retiring. I will have a very busy schedule. Between the local train and the express, I'm gonna brush. I brush between telephone calls. At the dance hall I brush. I don't dance on slow dances. I brush my hair while thinking about anything but mostly I think about how it will be when I get my full head of hair—like lifting my head in the morning will become a chore. I'll try to turn my cheek and my hair will weigh me down. I dream of Chaka Khan, chocolate from Grand Central Station with all seven wigs and Medusa. I brush and I brush. I use olive oil, hair food and Posner's Vitamin E, but mostly I brush and I brush. I may lose contact with most of my friends. I could lose my job, but I'm on unemployment and brush while waiting on line for my check. I'm sure I get good recommendations from my social worker, "Such a fastidious woman, that Lilly, always brushing her hair."

Nothing in my dreams suggests that hair brushing per se has anything to do with my particular head of hair. A therapist might say that the head full of hair has to do with something else, like a symbol of Lilly's unconscious desires, but I have no therapist. And my dreams mean things to me like, if you dream about Tobias then something has happened to Tobias, or he's gonna show up. If you dream about your grandma who's dead, than you must be doing something she doesn't like or she would not have gone to all that trouble to leave heaven like that. If you dream something red you should stop. If you dream something green you should keep on doing that. If a blue person appears in your dream, then that person is your true friend. And that's how I see my dreams.

And this head full of hair I have in my dreams is lavender and nappy as a three-year-old's in an apple tree. I can fry an egg and see the white of the egg spreading in the grease like my hair is gonna spread in the air. But I am not egg-yoke yellow, I am brown and the egg white is not white at all as actual hair, and it will go on and on forever, irregular like a Rastafarian man's hair. Irregular and gargantuan and lavender, nestled on blue satin pillows, pillows like the sky. And so I fry my eggs. I buy daisies, dyed lavender and lace lavender table mats and lavender nail polish.

Though I never admit it, I really do believe in magic, and can do strange things when something comes over me. Soon, everything around me will be lavender, fluffy and consuming. I will know not a moment of bitterness through all the wrist aching and tennis elbow from brushing. I'll smile. No regrets. "Je n'regrette rien" I'll sing, just like Edith Piaf. When my friends want me to go see Tina Turner or Pachecko I'll croon, "Sorry, I have to brush my hair."

I'll find ambrosia. My hair will grow pomegranates in soil rich as around the Aswan. I wake in my bed to bananas, avocados, collard greens, fresh croissant, Pouilly Fuissé, Ishmael Reed's essay, Charlotte Carter's stories, all just stream from my hair. And with the bricks that plop from where a nine-year-old's top braid would be, I will brush myself a house with running water and a bidet. I'll have a closet full of clean bed linen and a little girl from the Castro Convertible commercial will come and open the bed repeatedly and stay on as a helper to help me brush my hair.

I am the only person I know whose every word leaves a purple haze on the tip of your tongue. When this happens, I say clouds are forming and I have to close the windows. Violet rain is hard to remove from blue satin pillows.

ELIZABETH SPENCER

Elizabeth Spencer

The other day while wandering about, thinking obsessively about obsession, I passed a perfume counter in a store, and there it was, Obsession. Trapped in an array of oddly shaped bottles—flanked by "Passion" in purple bottles on one side and "Poison" in black bottles on the other. This seemed a fitting arrangement, as though a poet had devised it. Obsession. Passion. Poison. It's worthy of Baudelaire.

Martin Scorsese, remarking on his recent movie made of *The Age of Innocence*, saw its subject as obsession, which he described as an unattainable desire, a never-ending torment. He might have added that literature, like life, abounds in obsession. Ahab was obsessed with that whale. Quentin Compson was obsessed with his sister's honor. Silas Marner hated to lose his gold.

Obsession is like a virus. You don't seek it, but if you catch it, how do you lose it? Clearly there is a dark side to obsession, a diabolical darkness may be at work. The devil may be in it, and if he is, he's winning. Down goes the *Pequod*, all souls but one drown with her. Quentin Compson kills himself. I began to wonder if any light side is possible.

Then I found Ray Lum.

Ray Lum, no part Chinese, was born in 1891 in Vicksburg, Mississippi. He was a mule trader. During the major part of his life, mules were so attached to the farming landscape that if you didn't see mules, you didn't know if it was really a farm. Ray Lum was a trader and an auctioneer. He made private sales and public sales. He ranged through the Mississippi Delta and the hills. He knew everybody. His long life story is now in a book, a transcription of his very words, thick with his lived experience. This book is called *You Live and Learn, Then You Die and Forget it All.*

Through the decades of our century Ray Lum dealt in mules, not only in Mississippi and nearby states but also in Texas in the Southwest and bought wild horses by the thousands in South Dakota to ship south for sale. He traded and he swapped. He made money. "I never saw any place," he said, "where it was necessary to lie to a man in horse trades, but you handle the truth awful careful sometimes."

His trade was his obsession. He never gave it up. At age 85, during the 1970s, back in Vicksburg and sitting in his shop selling horse blankets and saddles, bridles and brushes, he was still attending every auction in a wide radius, though they were mainly in horses now, as mechanized farming had all but finished off the mule trade.

Ray Lum kept on because he couldn't quit. He bought up horses he couldn't even transport home, didn't need, and had no use to put them to. He would trade, acquire and leave them there. He was obsessed, but he was happily obsessed. He did not have tunnel vision. He wore no blinders on his bridle. It's this that makes him different.

Ray Lum remembered all the people he found in any way remarkable. He could tell about them all. He came too close to an ostrich once and it kicked him harder than a mule. He held the bets for a fight between a monkey and a bulldog. No lady speaking in the Folger Library should tell you how the monkey won. On a street out West he saw Pretty Boy Floyd. He was careful to look the other way. On a drive approaching Abilene in his "good Cadillac car," he gave a wide berth to Bonnie and Clyde, who were driving so fast all four wheels had left the ground.

It was not in spite of his obsession but because of it that Ray Lum lived a rich, fulfilled and loving life.

Why fall hopelessly in love with some trifling guy or some uncaring woman? Why spend your days

lusting for fame and fortune when you can do something really rewarding? Don't go chasing whales or worrying about your sister. If you have a choice, choose mules.

SCOTT SPENCER

Scott Spencer

Some years ago, I wrote *Endless Love*, which I wrote from the point of view of a love-starved and then love-sick young man. Though nowhere in the novel is the word Obsession used, I became, for a time, associated with the idea of obsession, and since then readers have found the theme of obsession in my work, as if I wrote about those whose moral dilemmas could be cured by psychiatry.

Obsession is one of those quasi-medical terms that have worn their way into the mainstream of language, and can appear and disappear like the Queen in a game of three-card-Monty. It is part of the language of control, a word we use against those whose actions we seek to govern. Sometimes, it seems whether or not you're an obsessive depends on crossing a very thin line. Fail to get a date with someone after asking her out a couple of times and you're a suitor; ask her out a third time—you're obsessed. Sometimes it means you just aren't looking out for number one. Speak out daily for the rights of the homeless and be given a salary to do so and you're a lobbyist; espouse the same views daily from a picket line and you're obsessed. And sometimes it means you're living by some unfashionable credo, a degraded Commandment. A man who says he will do literally anything to protect his family has a good chance of being described as a model father; a man who says we will do literally anything to protect that nice family who lives next door will probably find himself described as obsessed, and may be directed to seek counseling. Collect string and you're an obsessive; collect Renaissance art and you're...a collector.

On the political level, we have seen the elusiveness of obsession's definition in the past couple of years. Whereas once anti-communism was routinely considered patriotic, even mandatory, this former mainstay of American political consciousness is now looked on as a kind of feverish derangement.

A recent issue of the *St. Petersburg Times* (in Florida, not Russia) said, "the fall of the Soviet Union has freed the US from a national psychosis. Our irrational obsession with communism dominated our collective unconscious as surely as any phobic disorder." The writer may be correct, but what we have here is not the sharpening of a political analyses, but a shift in power relations. Today we're selling light bulbs to the Hungarians and Mrs. Butterworth's Breakfast Syrup to the Ukraine. Business with the Eastern Bloc is Renaissance art and, now, espousing anti-communism is like collecting string.

Calling an act **obsessive** is society's way of shouting ENOUGH. And now, in our co-dependent, dysfunctional age—the language of control is medical. Just as we label as paranoia the fears of those who are powerless and whose view of reality we do not respect, so do we brand obsessive those people whose passions are inconvenient, or too long-lived, or too sexual, too costly, too dangerous, or too critical of the current consensus.

And it is here, in that vast public ward implied by the word obsession, that the characters in my novels are forced to take their meals—with stalkers, rapists, and disgruntled former employees. Is it any wonder that I look forward to the time when the word Obsession collapses under the weight it has been asked to bear, when it will become a diagnosis as antique as the Vapors?

This first edition of *Obsession* is
published for PEN/Faulkner Foundation
by Quill & Brush in an edition of
600 copies in paperwraps.
In addition, there are
200 numbered hardbound copies & 44 deluxe
copies (26 lettered & 18 for presentation) signed by
each of the authors. These copies also include a
signed original silk screen
by Lou Stovall.

Copy 70